The Navigator and the Explorer

Also by Adrian Rogers and published by Ginninderra Press
The Sun Behind the Sun
Between Two Hemispheres
The Prisoner's Messenger
The Medicine Wheel
Music is a River of Life
A Way Less Travelled
Ecce Homo
Pamir
Seasons, Situations and Symbols (Pocket Poets)
Flowers and Star Signs (Pocket Poets)
Human Nature & the Welfare State (Pocket Polemics)
Croagh Patrick (Pocket Places)
Port Victoria (Pocket Places)

Adrian Rogers

The Navigator and the Explorer

The Navigator and the Explorer
ISBN 978 1 76109 545 0
Copyright © text Adrian Rogers 2023
Cover image: Golden Leo

First published 2023 by
GINNINDERRA PRESS
PO Box 3461 Port Adelaide 5015
www.ginninderrapress.com.au

Contents

Introduction	7
Part 1: The Navigator	
Looking Back – November 1909	11
The Adventure Begins – 24 April 1895	12
Night Sail	14
Gibraltar	15
Amazonia/Mother	16
Coasting South	17
The Terrible Straits	18
Watcher of the Seas	19
Pacific Voyaging	20
Dreaming Between Islands and a Continent	22
Mother India's Ocean	23
Rounding the Cape	24
Into the Doldrums	25
On the Home Run – 1899	26
Between the Pillars…1909	27
Part 2: The Explorer (From His Diary)	
Prologue – Written on the Flyleaf	31
Leaf 1 – Probing the Mystery	32
Leaf 2 – The Call	33
Leaf 3 – Searching	34
Leaf 4 – Towards the Source	35
Leaf 5 – 'If We Do Not Return Let No Rescue Be Sent'	36
Leaf 6 – Tributary Crossing	37
Leaf 7 – Dead Horse Camp, (Mind Games)	38
Leaf 8 – The Last Letter (Interpreted)	39
Leaf 9 – We Three (The Vow)	40
Afterwards – A Personal Reflection	41

Part 3: The Summons Takes Flight

Wing/Wave Turnaway	45
An Explorer Reflects	46
Jungle – Illusion or Reality	47
Back, Then Forward Seven Steps	48
Stranger	49
The Long Wave	50
Two and One	51
An Explorer, and the Lore	52
Prophetic Light Flashes	53
The Mariner's Summons	55
The Explorer's Summons	56
The Final Summons	57

Introduction

There is a first time for everything, and for sailing around the world alone that honour belongs to Captain Joshua Slocum, a Canadian-born seaman who circumnavigated the globe between 1895 and 1899. Everyone knew this had been done often enough, but no one before Slocum had done it alone – let alone in a converted oyster fishing boat named *Spray*. Returning to Boston in 1899, he wrote a book about his experiences, but after that, what more could there be? This much we do know: he set sail for the West Indies in 1909 and was never seen again.

Colonel Percy Fawcett, soldier, cartographer and explorer, was convinced that a great civilisation once existed in the remotest parts of the Brazilian rainforest, which he was intent on finding. Fawcett was a theosophist, and Theosophy teaches that Divine knowledge may be achieved by spiritual ecstasy, direct intuition or individual relationships. Membership of the Theosophical Society is surely a strange qualification for an explorer, so what was he really seeking? He, like Slocum disappeared, in 1926 on his last foray into the jungle.

The achievements of these great men are reflected in parts 1 and 2 of this collection, while in part 3, flights of fancy look sideways at their achievements.

Adrian Rogers

Part 1

The Navigator

Looking Back – November 1909

Sea voices never far
are a mind's first and last
sleep echoers
long-shoreline breaking
hissing, murmurous,
a still-felt ocean lift, roll,
wind-shake howling
a cold salt spray,
but in life now, an ebb tide
and no more rising
my star, of its polar home
bereft untried like driftwood,
a pride in circumnavigation
solo forgotten,
on an empty beach, my keel
wave-riding no longer
as time, stronger
drains the wine cup of memory.

My boat, ageing
off-centres hope
yet I remember ice
colliding mindlessly sharp
to dismember
with Antarctic breath, yet
may there be
another deed of note
laid to my charge if I obey
unwritten, the summoning,
a final valediction?

The Adventure Begins – 24 April 1895

This time was strong, enchanted,
at my side hope venturing
hearing, unlimiting in scope
voices, glances of those
fearing to abide
a moment of the infinite, feeling
Atlantic's sun-flashing
dancing wave break,
knowing that rise-fall rolling
catch, a sharp salt sting
as ocean beckoned
herself flaunted
but never daunted familial pods
of porpoise, dolphin, seal
and whale balletic, enhancing
counterpointed bird-calls
chorusing my *Spray*
as she, pirouetting
overrode breakers
chancing the nay-sayers
the dream-shakers to ride
long-sloped rollers far from land,
for I had tied my hopes
re-fashioned to forget
a passive coasting oyster boat,

she now would face the deeps
laughingly defy
potentially exploding
crested waves depth-sounding as I
dared to sail
around the world alone
sharing with none the summons;

'So be it!' I heard you, ocean,
I answered.

Night Sail

In a heart subduing night's
restrained sea-restiveness
clarity held sway,
thin-cresting lines like the whites
of eyes thin-glittering

and time, never away frittering
saw *Spray* overrunning
sotto voce depths, soundings
outriding
moon/star glancing wavetops
driving alert
intuitional perceiving

no storm disturbing
this momentary livingness
sight-lengthening into darkness,
muttering
hull caressing water rushes
while I, universally at one
with those measured-long
Atlantic nights
saw past, future, and eternity
as now.

Gibraltar

Ocean, examiner impartial
exempts none, all tested
as was I
wave/wind slapped
side-to-side whipped
capricious
questioning, initiated,
compacted
by impressions asserting
Gibraltar
from grey-sheened bright
wave-patterns
swaying into light
and jumble-clustered dark
hill masses rising
blunt-edged aspiring
to a peak overseeing
a harbour walled under bleak
sculpted rock faces
steel-grey sea
under the disapproving gaze
of empire…

but for such pomp of desire
let be *'till the captains
and the kings depart'*.

Amazonia/Mother

The sea, somnolent blue/lit
saw the boat scarce lift
on a swell's minimal drift
enhancing
a flying fish silver/pearl
leaping
from depths blue-shadowed
sun-veiled, water-wild,
consciousness alerted
off the starboard beam
to dark forest lines
dream-greened intensified
fearing not
a yellow-fevered swamp

where Amazonia's stamp
force-rushed continental waters
oceanward
birth-blood stained
to current-sacrificing power,
my boat stirring
echoed sun-hot shimmering
moveless air salt-tasted
dispersed
by drummed ritual offerings
breeze-caught
while I, turned south sought
no intrusions
just a cat's-paw, breathed
beyond mystery.

Coasting South

Above a headland fire
flame-fingering downward
through shadowed tree cover
smoke/drift/hazed
then afterward
from fire to flood
a wreckage of desire, again
the blood of sacrifice,

a wind offshore, an attire
of billowing sails
discouraged unfazed intruding
when southward turned
I followed the seal's way
drawn not back
from the shark's fin track
triangular, secretive
in his bow wave tracing
and wake
my passage marking
light flare and shake
gulls white-flecking the day
beyond smoke drift
over bay and inlet
heart's lift and wave break
south-away.

The Terrible Straits

Claws, teeth, water
and fire-dragon testing,
I recalled
that terrible strait's
fierce lightning-whiteness
darkening seas streaked
foaming, roaring
a whirling forcefield
Magellan,
your cross-over mistress
and lover self-mirrored
ice-fingered, goaded
to be or not to be
undaunted,
a power upholding me
when terror was
in the standing wave
the node
a south/north reaching
yet beseeching power
water-firing
a sharp-rocked blading
raiding velocity
strong though loath
almost, by desiring
wind roar, spray-whip,
turmoil and thunder flash
as I, in the raging a name,
a moment,
a dash paged-in by destiny
became immortal.

Watcher of the Seas

Dark sea slumber's Pacific starred afterwards
was the I, offloading a lumbering storm stress
yet this I, haunted by post-tempest sickness

daunted on a single note, a quaver-flit
scored by destiny forwards, backwards
became, from everyway prevented

by incipient weakness yet a-flutter in strength,
afloat with resolve from a delirious day-night
thralldom's

consanguinity, discontented, awaiting revival
to a fullness slow-involving away-backed hopes,
fighting fear's Imperium, staggering in darkness

onto my deck, temporising on a new manhood,
an invented half-forming fearlessness
against a night sky soaring gold-spangled

star spray, seeing a watcher guiding my boat
towards dawn.

'Stranger, by wonder am I shorn, speculating
on the who, the why, the what…you are.'

Pacific Voyaging

Spray, my sail-winged
soul-winged leaper,
her preference
the steadier swell/sweeps
shied away
from the Roaring Forties
seeking winds softened
persuasive
rather than a prevailing
Mater Pacifica, ringing
the changes toned
deeper, nosing
into scented breezes
sidling in tacking mode,
dreaming unbroken.

'O Albatross, my friend
may you suffer no loss
from the curse of ignorant
long-line fishers
confluent with the dross
of greed and insecurity.'

Your sun-brushing wings
tailed my progress
on a star-paled regress
into dawn, till south-away
turning you rode out
a storm-long almost
year-long tyranny,
yet you and I knew not
that Inner Sun
behind the Sun, source
point of singularity.

Dreaming Between Islands and a Continent

Between light-hazing
shimmer-shake and dipping
green-jeweled islands
I, inshore lifting glimmer-
dreaming a gaze, slipping
my lead-line soundings
feared not a lee shore
sensing heat only
rising to enervate
or elevate my lotus musings.

To starboard, palms
emerald-glowing-tinted,
light overspreading
shifted slightly,
while away to port
the Great South Land
seemed lazily dreaming
its insouciant illusions.

Did the new understand
the old,
both live and thrive
with the gold of memory
in the dormancy
of a great Southern Land?

A sun-yellow afternoon
stretched itself
in passing.

Mother India's Ocean

Mother India, ocean voices
wind/wave summoning
could not command
the self's identifying
progression in the wake
of a past, to futures
at my bow wave risen
from the grave of self-doubt,
south-west turned
into memory's recessional
reaches into being.

Hope, never spurned
took flight revealing
all, at day's breaking despite
a dream-shaking
Leviathan threatening
from beaches self-stranded
yet did I not, bereft
fear depths darkening
blue/green/black,
or mysteries
no choices proffering,
setting fast my course
dead reckoning
on Good Hope's beckoning.

Rounding the Cape

Clouds like white smoke
billowing, draped themselves
like an amplitude of incense
over Table Mountain's
half-distant clarity
sun-shadowing
my *Spray* pitching,
swing-toss catching wavetop
scatter flicked-flinging
sun-tipped flashings blue-sided,
tracking the ghost
of Vasco da Gama in reverse

responding to the obverse,
wind strength variable
like Africa's fortunes,
changeable
moodily impressionistic
infrangible
and like swerving
wave-contour dancing birds
unpredictable

as I, successively gradual
turned *Spray's* bow
tacking, lifting strong
into my Atlantic-mother's
wind-song long-swell-riding
harmony, chill,
salt-tasting, but of home.

Into the Doldrums

Prospective calls of sea-storm
and winds contrary
somehow less demanding
than searchingly
spiritual Atlantic challenges
haunting still
my half-wild dreams
and devising schemes
off-course blown
along the skeleton coast,
while the wind, sewn
by night time-fired faery
water-dancers
countermanded desires
controlled,
until into doldrums lurching
aspiration died with the wind.

Concentric forces thinned
uninspiringly,
floated me above depth
and mystery
seeking a formless 'what',
making me in tropical heat
less than a dot
impressed on perceptions
unchallenged.

On the Home Run – 1899

Initiated by water, fire,
and the standing wave
homing – no absolution
was for a roaming heart
tempted again to depart
in the wake of Ulysses
ambitious for immortality,
but my dreaming
perhaps a self-scheming
circumnavigating
deeming, yet abiding

though little desiring
the home run since
what was done
was done as *Spray*
ploughed north by west
accepting with little zest
wave-break
and starboard buffeting
without surrendering
captured only by Atlantic's
bustling trade routes,
homeward turning
towards achievement's
seaward breakwater
outthrust, weed-coated,
but not rusted on the soul
as yet…

Between the Pillars...1909

Light-sparking-gold polished drops
polka-dot blue/green waves
beyond the breakwater...

the dust of centuries is falling softly

onto long-line hooks of ambition,
and Ulysses again
soul conditioning, destined
from the circled centre
unto the ineffable beyond...

'ashes to ashes, dust to dust',

by grace not daunting or corroding
before the Pillars of Eternity
dark wave looming,
a confraternity wind-song gusted
salt tasted, unfulfillable
or perhaps not, because...

the dust of centuries is falling softly.

Beyond cold petrification
there may be
some deed of note
laid to my charge if I obey
the final summoning...

the dust of centuries is falling softly.

Part 2

The Explorer (From His Diary)

Prologue – Written on the Flyleaf

I am the dark, the green
and shadowed light,
not another
seeking wealth
stolen by force or stealth
from my brother

a secret voice
a town crier, advocating
the adversarial fellowship
of wildness,
a red blue green/yellowing
faceted glowing mystery
culled…
from unutterable history
downcasting no other
nor smothering the quest
for meaning since fame
though not demeaning
seeds coldness,
yet boldness
speaks truth to power.

I will not cower
before the gods of the West
or strain the curds of regret
but pay my debt,
shaping things to come.

Leaf 1 – Probing the Mystery

Where, in the green heart
impenetrable
do the rivers rise?

Memories play a part,
not lies but winged tales
rainbow coloured
ring/patterned
light shafted, filtered
through jungle/shadowed
breathing heat pulsed
seething like a pot
bubbling
where river veins
life-blooded/water-flooded
stir consciousness,
merge…
perception the driver
in a momentary surge.

Dark, light, shadow
and sigh mark
each fearful instant, fight
an urge to tarry, let go
a mystery's calling
because hidden, not lost
a city, a civilisation,
earth changes,
a technology of spirit;

these must I seek.

Leaf 2 – The Call

Outed, by a dark restlessness
of night-bird call echoes
vibrated
through blackness palpable
into light rays
fingering a jungle canopy
skin-mottling the power play
of an anaconda
spotted-tawny patterning
a jaguar patrolling
merciless yet wary
as rainbow-jewel flashings
of the parrot kind,

swamping foulness blind
oozing rot, flows,
alligator-like intenseness
lurking an intangibility
contrapuntal
as *Days of Our Lives* trivia
dream-sunk in a boiling
fixated mind's groundswell
unstilled…

all is memory, a filled
mind against materiality
launched
into the dawn-river light.

Leaf 3 – Searching

Dipping slicking paddles
dawn-lit drive
brown hulled boats
silvering through waters
riverine
flash-flushing dreams
without doubt
yet swarmed by doubts
and uncertainty bouts
on channels wild-wide
banked green
forest dark, still distantly
a fired surging brightness
as I sense
sacred headwaters
ending and beginning,
falls plunging
from the urgent finalising
of rock-shadowed faces
searching densities
shadow-greened-alive
intensities, until
stone-formed pillars
somewhere
image-carved are found
while I, unbound
will not share,
deconsecrate a mystery
or desecrate before
the gods of capital
sacredness everywhere.

Leaf 4 – Towards the Source

Off the main channel
wet tactile
jungle green ferocity
hems us in
along waterways narrowing
a 'pilgrim's progress'
harrowing, while guile
guiding stress-tried forces
drives us towards the prize
distance glowing,
or a frozen grey rock
looming, a shock,
the doom of discovery
through trees crowding
shrouding yet revealing
the natural, or manmade.

Making the grade
demands emergence
through jostling hopes,
fears of the poisonous,
mazes vegetative
frustrations, tears, minding
what springs eternal,
hope…finding
the origin of all things.

'Let there be light!'

Leaf 5 – 'If We Do Not Return Let No Rescue Be Sent'

One man on the Orinoco
found fool's gold,
not sold am I
on El Dorado dreams
of avarice
and none
trialing vile schemes
shall touch
the inconceivable secrets
of eternity.

I am a calling beyond verifying
which will burn
past this material life
pursuing the lost
at any personal cost
hearing
a voice I know, a too
great for the many
unity self-uttering silently
therefore, to honour my intent…

If we do not return
let no rescue be sent.

Leaf 6 – Tributary Crossing

Setting out from Cuiaba
in the dawn light
sun-flares dazzling
slick-silver river/current
flows turn, turning swirling
Children of the Sun
every-which-way
coming and going
somewhere
rhythmic paddles sparking
diamantine,
the in-closing jungle
riotously green/gold/shot
shadowing loud
everywhere
rainbow-parroting voices
beak-heavy hornbills
loudly invisible swarms
concentrated insectile, until
in passing a tributary
slow-time crosses
those hours anywhere

my boat is shadowed, light
flash-cuts flare
spasmodically
afloat on black waters
channeling that
'Dance of the Hours,' at this
Tributary Crossing.

Leaf 7 – Dead Horse Camp (Mind Games)

I have traced this river's course
to a shadowed source...

pounding drums
sounding ambiguities, reasons,
'Signs of the Times'
in half-awake rhymes...for
all Seasons'?

I, Son of the Widow guard
the approaching processional
Six Pillared Way
to the Centre, for which
I leave this track recessional
lacking the seasoning
of logical thought
stretching minds
on the rack of vision...

but on the shadow's far side
the unutterable secrets of eternity
are...from the desperados
of our age kept, so,
at Dead Horse Camp
we build a ramp against doubt,
though my horse died as we
pitched our evening tents.

What will become of us?

Leaf 8 – The Last Letter (Interpreted)

The river slides between tangled roots,
green-waved overhanging
drooping branches deflect
sun-flash, star, moonlight
and whispering voices
of spirit flutes,
expectation darkening
self-sings into jungle trances
one last time
none barring from inner sight
the secretive outcomes of our choices.

Others have found great civilisations
plumbed past mysteries,
yet more awaits
than febrile concentrations
of materially has-been histories.

Wait for me before destiny's gates,
I shall be gone but a while
not by foreboded time/woven fates
but in time returning
across time burning
the fires of ages, so let it be…

we will share the secrets of eternity.

Leaf 9 – We Three (The Vow)

'We three are bonded, to seek and find
the inviolable secrets of eternity, bind

with fidelity ourselves to the quest
for wisdom from flame to source, invest

our search for the ultimate with austerity
outreaching the absolute, sincerity

of purpose devoid of contamination,
an exacting conscience examination

and consciousness elevation. They call
us from darkness, light, the spiralling fall

of a leaf, voices of jungles, waterways
slipping silently past and by, nights, days

sun, cloud, rained, thunderstruck, yet still
true of voice. Let be what must be, we will

prevail; this is our choice…'

Afterwards – A Personal Reflection

Water, and light flashing
are not the same
as when we turned away
from clasped hands
as they left, and the jungle
crowding closed
green-shadow curtaining
chattering bird calls
and river whisperings
trailing the departed 'three'
leaving us, held only
by a silence of the heart.

Memory stranded, a part
of history's night-to-day
game is – with us
parting not the warp
weft and weave of destiny,
but validating the quest
for those incommunicable
secrets of eternity
known only
to a sacred fraternity

beyond echoing…for those
seeing not the river
as before,
light, water/life giving, even
the jungle so forgetting
…or has it?

Are they truly taken,
brothers in immortality?

Part 3

The Summons Takes Flight

Wing/Wave Turnaway

I turn away
from a steel/grey cold
exacting Southern Ocean's
long/high wave lengths
yellow scud-whipped
northwest
into Pacific moderation
bidding
my wandering albatross
a friend's farewell
on his swept/wing white
wide southward arcing
wheeling back
to storm wild seas,
yet from these
my boat's bowsprit
points me to blue-sloped
sun-gold waters
silver-flashed flying fish
spouting whales
and the swift black/white
piratical frigate bird.

This call I heard
and hear again as sails fill
into long-lit strong-lit days.

An Explorer Reflects

Our lives are shadows
fleeting
in all but memory
tending desire,
our garden of discontent
blooms in the rays
of inspiration, its fires
their shining light
a higher self-illuminating.

Let not egoic possessing
cut the Tree of Life
harrowing
our consciousness
and let it not disbar
that truest quality of self,
a self-initiating.

Jungle – Illusion or Reality

Water, linking me
with the astral plane
sweeps over and into
bodily substance, sweat
and, in the outer
gifted by jungle creepers
face touching fronds
moss and bark
seen as though through
a glass, dark…

with truth implanted
into perception, a debt
to materiality for a doubter
though – like a stone
one self-isolated is more,
and when a machete
hacks creepers sacrificially
aside tearing, my blade
grates, dropping a watery
shower like confetti.

Is this a scored writing
etched, just hands
ageing, a theosophy
of timeliness, or knowledge
timelessly given?

What am I really seeking?

Back, Then Forward Seven Steps

The road long, serpentine
was now a sharp incline
seven stepped
to a light crowned summit
and the spear shaker, his remit
The Spear of Destiny cast
between the Sunset's Gates

after a syncline/anticline way
hard-scoped, visionary,
awaiting an intensity
of longing's constancy
seeing those gates
pierce an evening sky vast
red/gold, a dark, translucent
moment, the Spear
passing at the last between
stark pillars as,
standing before a sun/moon
conjoining revelation
we, and they
sought a correlation, All,
and One.

Stranger

She sways in the dark
my cabin lift-lilting
tilting and returning
as hazed hours I mark
daunted by sickness,
distance, fear haunting
an instance aware,
a vast defiance of reality
driving me
emerging, staggering
seeing spark/fire stars,
feeling a surge
as they swing across
the heavens
and oneness leavens
my seeing.

Sails and taught spars
frame a watcher
tall against a night sky
sweep-turning
star/fire bars of light…

'Stranger, who are you?'

The Long Wave

This long-low-lifting
is a slumberous timespan
self-extended, yet rifting
masked awareness
to where a leap will save
the flash-flying fish,
no wingspan needed
but wide-fins wave-gifting
a momentary sureness
beyond hope, fearlessness
and memory long lit
amid bird cries
at the sun turning
blue to gold.

Wind sighs foretell nights
burning
ongoing into days marked
by the Trident sign
into dawn light rising
on my bowsprit's
aspiring
towards sea-sprayed light.

Two and One

A flame in the dark, small light, a game
of thrones, tones resonating, changing

dance steps as night draws on, ranging
in search of solar enlightenment, the goal

a summer light at rest illuminating a soul
treasuring mystery in-depth-luminous

and lastingly inward, a veil voluminous
yet, for an approaching wanderer only

an anchorage infinitely calm, lonely,
memorable, an introspective stillness

for the keel; love on the heart as a seal,
one yet all under the sun for lovers

themselves true, free from shadow-shake
and storm, knowing joy after heartbreak.

An Explorer, and the Lore

A jungle's green-to-rooted self
grasps at the river yet backsteps
from its force,
scarce wilting despite the heat's
enveloping
water over land daylong
in a light-scape's enigma, strong,
encompassing
green, blue, red, a display
heraldic of parroting songsters
and beating jungle rhythms
code-like proclaiming
lore and laws
inflexibly enforceable.

Branch, leaf, frond, graspable
as vine and shadow
cloak vegetating flourishes
overwhelming
whomever would clear a path,
unbar the way to the lost
for a soul lost in itself…

by the mystery of the jaguar's
spotted shadowing,
enwinding things creeping
and a secretively closing way,
is the beginning the end?

Prophetic Light Flashes

Leaping
against the sun's rising
running-wave-mountain
blue flinging your white crest
against the light
crash into dissolution
only to return.

Creeping
spiralling, up-risen green
seeking youth's fountain,
let the bells ring
at love's behest
against the might of negation
resolving, as life's guest
to celebrate and sing.

Sleeping,
or unenterprising
wake to a siren-wave song,
out-shake
the foam from your hair,
be a singing light,
zest in discovery, finding
in a fern's sound-tracing
a revolution.

By the One and the Three
to be, wave lifted
or found
in the depths of the sea,
'Poussin Teniers
guard the Key'
to the lost, unbound,
not under a tree
but a green mound
where light is drawn down
from the sun.

The Mariner's Summons

Small pebbles sharpen sand
shallow-sloped underfoot
and skies blue
to cloud-grey wind harried
seem infinite
yet all, illusory, finite
challenges the day
on a wave subduing strand
when the navigator
obeying a late summoning
grounds the keel
in stillness, a shoreline
destiny inevitable

yet memory, inflexible
as timed coral spawning
white-lit-pale-coloured
chiming moonstruck rising
through black water
mirrors translucence, above
and below
a half-clouded sky
enacting oceanic magic
swayed, by
impersonal transience.

The Explorer's Summons

Explorer, catch the link
shimmering a green leaf
to the sea
between moonlight and
and a coral-spawned wonder,
a fruit dropped
in jungle quietude
or rain drenched thunder
unto light, dark, passing on

finding the glass castle,
seeing
a rainbow about the throne,
an emerald,
a crystalline ocean
beyond endless worlds.

By the sons of morning
summoned
to the halls of Annwm,
by the Harp of Tara
finding your end
in your beginning, and
at every bend in the road
a degree, become
yourself by the waters
in silence, a step closer
to being…

The Final Summons

When opposites meet
on the shore
under sky rain-shadowing
a mystery
until the overcast becomes
at the last a rainbow
arching
'Tel of the obelisks'
linking
and sons of a widow
are summoned
to venture on dark waters
mirroring,
following the Spear's flight…

'I am, as air, light,
a soul's refinement
rendered
by The Mills of God
finding
on twin pillars terrestrial
and celestial secrets,
knowing
when the lost is found
by a lamp
that the time has come.'

www.ingramcontent.com/pod-product-compliance
Lightning Source LLC
Chambersburg PA
CBHW071037080526
44587CB00015B/2652